*Quick*GUIDES

everything you need to know...fast

Vision and Mission Statements

by **Helen Carter**
reviewed by Katie Roebuck

WIREMILL
PUBLISHING LTD

Across the world the organizations and institutions that fundraise to finance their work are referred to in many different ways. They are charities, non-profits or not-for-profit organizations, non-governmental organizations (NGOs), voluntary organizations, academic institutions, agencies, etc. For ease of reading, we have used the term Nonprofit Organization, Organization or NPO as an umbrella term throughout the *Quick*Guide series. We have also used the spellings and punctuation used by the author.

Published by
Wiremill Publishing Ltd.
Edenbridge, Kent TN8 5PS, UK
info@wiremillpublishing.com
www.wiremillpublishing.com
www.quickguidesonline.com

British Library Cataloguing in Publication Data
A catalogue record for this book is available from the British Library.

ISBN Number 1-905053-40-1

Printed by Rhythm Consolidated Berhad, Malaysia
Cover Design by Jennie de Lima and Edward Way
Design by Colin Woodman

CONTENTS

INTRODUCTION

These days, everyone seems to have a Vision Statement. But how many of your colleagues know your organisation's Vision and Mission? How does it connect to everyday work?

Following are some examples of major corporate organisations' Vision and Mission Statements that encompass a holistic view.

- "To be Canada's Premier Diamond Producer, creating a legacy of Responsible Safety, Environmental and Employee-Development Practice and Enduring Community Benefit."

- "The aim of the Royal Dutch/Shell Group is to meet the energy needs of society, in ways that are economically, socially and environmentally viable, now and in the future."

- "To be a great Australasian company – a great place to work, a superior customer experience, 1st-quartile shareholder returns, a good corporate citizen."

But what about nonprofit organisations? How can Vision and Mission Statements help them? When organisations are in business to "save the environment" or "fight cancer," is there any reason for them to say anything more about what they do?

This Guide offers a way of thinking about your organisation's Vision and Mission. Questions are posed to help you decide if you need a Vision Statement, who should be involved in developing it, and what happens after you've come up with one.

Reviewer's Comment

Missions and Visions explain why you are here, where you want to get to, and how you will do it. They are communication and planning tools which enable those both inside and outside your organisation to understand how you see both the present and the future.

Defining Vision, Mission, Values and Plans

Every organisation should decide what the words "Vision, Mission, Values and Plans" mean to it. Establishing a common understanding of these terms in the early stages is important. Just as every organisation could interpret the meaning of the terms in different ways, so can individuals within your organisation. But don't spend too much time on the definitions – it's the intention that matters most.

Defining the meaning of these terms is the first step in creating a Vision, and the definitions will most likely be discussed and agreed on by the Board (the governing body of the organisation) and Chief Executive (the most senior staff member of your organisation). Of course, not all organisations have paid staff, in which case the task will fall to volunteers.

There is no universally correct definition of a Vision. Sometimes Vision and Mission are interchangeable and sometimes they are one and the same.

One way of looking at how Vision, Mission, Values and Plans work together is by thinking about the parts of a car.

- The Vision is the headlights – they shed light on the road ahead.

- The Mission is the engine – what keeps you going.

- The Values are the wheels – they support everything else.

- The Plans are the steering wheel and gears – what give you control.

Here are some definitions and examples.

Mission – the purpose of your organisation. The Mission usually doesn't change much over time. For example:

- The Mission of an animal shelter might be "We are committed to saving the lives of animals."

- "We are passionate about raising awareness of X (issue or need)."

Vision – what your organisation wants to achieve, usually within a particular time frame. A Vision can be reviewed and changed as your organisation progresses. For example:

- "In one year, our shelter will be the first place where people come to adopt a pet."

- "In four years, we will be internationally recognised as a leading source of knowledge on X."

Continues on next page

Values – the beliefs that your organisation is founded on. For example:

■ "We believe that all animals have a right to protection from harm. We support our staff in their ability to achieve our Vision by providing a safe work environment and appropriate training. We run our shelter in collaboration with our community and we value its support."

■ "We are committed to raising awareness of X by offering quality resources and information to our communities. We strongly value our volunteers and financial partners and, as an independent organisation, do not accept government or corporate funding."

Plans – consist of three parts: (1) a list of things you want to achieve (outcomes), (2) the things you are going to do to achieve them (actions), and (3) the ways you will know that you have achieved them (measures). For example:

■ More dogs are adopted (outcomes).

■ Advertise in the local media and secure a celebrity to be our patron (actions).

■ The number of dogs adopted doubled in 12 months (measures).

■ Enquiries for seminars on X increased (outcomes).

■ Networking was done with local government and community organisations (actions).

■ There was a 30 percent increase in the number of seminars held, and evaluation forms show 85 percent positive feedback (measures).

Your organisation might already have different definitions for these terms, but for this Guide, the definition of Vision is what an organisation wants to achieve and by when.

The Vision is the foundation for everything your organisation will do over the next five to 10 years. It has to be achievable and aspirational. If your Vision is set too far into the future, the people in your organisation will not connect with it. Most people want to be able to celebrate a major organisational achievement; at the same time, they want to be able to do it in a realistic time frame. The world is a dynamic place, and organisations are dynamic as well. A Vision that is set 20 years ahead will most likely be irrelevant within 10 years.

Defining Vision, Mission, Values and Plans

If you are an environmental organisation and your Vision is "to be the biggest online environmental campaigner in 25 years," this Vision is probably looking too far ahead. A more realistic Vision might be "to have 10,000 online environmental campaigners within one year."

Depending on its size, an organisation might have a number of Vision Statements that support the achievement of its Mission. Usually an organisational Vision Statement will be the first to be developed, followed by department Visions. Department Visions will directly support the achievement of the organisational Vision.

Some organisations use their Plans to express department goals, rather than write department Vision Statements. There's no right or wrong way to structure your Vision, Mission, Values and Plans. What is important is that you create what you need in order to achieve your Mission, and that you avoid using complex structures to communicate the what, why, how and who of your organisation.

A Note on Mission Statements

As noted above, a Mission Statement defines the purpose of your organisation. It is usually short and specific to what you do. The Mission Statement will probably not change over time and will continue to guide the more dynamic Vision Statements. However, the process for developing and reviewing a Mission Statement can be similar to the process for developing Vision Statements. The key to developing a living Mission Statement is making sure the people who are important to your organisation have the chance to participate in the development of the Mission Statement. The Mission Statement is what prospective customers, staff or clients will look to first to see what your organisation is all about. A clear and strong Mission Statement can also be used to reinforce the organisation's purpose internally. The Mission Statement is the initial call to action and the great motivator.

Reviewer's Comment
By being aspirational, a Vision Statement can challenge an organisation to stretch itself to achieve more.

THE VALUE OF A VISION STATEMENT

There are many examples of how a good Vision Statement can help an organisation improve how well it uses its resources, how well it manages and values its people, how well it is regarded by others in the outside world, and how innovative it is.

A great Vision Statement:

■ Can set your organisation apart by describing how it is unique. This can help improve how well your organisation is recognised in the community, or make the difference to someone considering your service or product over someone else's.

■ Will make your organisation become more effective and efficient at what it does, thus preserving valuable resources, because everyone knows where they're going and why.

■ Can attract donors and make it easier for those involved in fundraising to tell the story of your organisation.

■ Can help attract the right people to work for your organisation.

■ Can inspire people to advocate for your organisation.

■ Can express the organisation's Values. This is particularly important to many nonprofit organisations.

Creating and then reviewing a Vision Statement:

■ Can be a great way of bringing the different areas of your organisation together to work more effectively.

■ Can help people feel that they have a voice and are valued (therefore reducing recruiting costs).

■ Can strengthen your organisational family; that is, people will feel united by a common goal.

■ Can be fun, offering a chance for people to talk to others about what the organisation means to them.

■ Can allow time for people to reflect on where your organisation is going and how it will get there.

■ Can establish meaningful reasons for regular discussion about such things as the future and what's going on outside of your organisation that might have an impact on your Vision, and provide a forum for recognition of achievement and innovation.

THE VALUE OF A VISION STATEMENT

The process of developing a Vision Statement can also help your organisation focus or provide stability during times of change. When the going gets tough, a strong Vision Statement whose intention is shared can reinforce the purpose of your organisation.

An organisation's Values might come from a particular religious affiliation or from one person's dream to create a better world. Whatever the source, your Vision must come from being passionate about what your organisation wants to achieve. Of course, having a clearly stated Mission at the outset is useful, but Visions can be achieved on their own.

Some examples of Vision or Mission Statements that are clear and inspiring follow.

■ **Greenpeace International**

"Greenpeace is an independent, campaigning organisation that uses non-violent, creative confrontation to expose global environmental problems, and force solutions for a green and peaceful future. Greenpeace's goal is to ensure the ability of the Earth to nurture life in all its diversity."

■ **World Vision Australia**

"In Serving Christ, we commit ourselves to engaging people in transforming lives by alleviating poverty and confronting its causes."

■ **Google**

"Google's Mission is to deliver the best search experience on the Internet by making the world's information universally accessible and useful."

Reviewer's Comment
Vision Statements can galvanise people into action – they add life and emotion to an often dry Mission, and can encourage "out of the box" solutions to the challenges an organisation may face.

Some organisations have their Visions thrust upon them by getting Board members (Directors, Trustees or Governors) together on a Saturday afternoon to come up with a catchy-sounding slogan. The unfortunate Chief Executive is then left to somehow implement this Vision, maybe by sending out a newsletter or an email to let everyone know what the new Vision is. This approach will probably not give an organisation the results it wants.

One reason that Vision Statements are met with indifference is because they simply are not relevant to the very people who need to make them a reality. People feel more passionate about things that matter to them, that they have some say about, and over which they have some control. This is the challenge for a leader when creating a Vision.

An important consideration is determining who you want to involve in the process. For example:

- The governing Board
- Senior staff
- Those people who benefit from your service
- Representatives from supporter groups
- Funding bodies
- Elected staff representatives

When selecting members of your working group, ask yourself this question: Who do we want to be committed to or supportive of the work of our organisation? Who is going to make our Vision a reality?

Reviewer's Comment
The Vision has to be "owned" by the whole organisation – by people from all groups and at all levels. If it isn't, it can sound false and hollow, and it can highlight conflicts within an organisation.

Consensus in Developing Vision

It is crucial to know what the organisation wants to get out of the Vision exercise.

Does the Chief Executive or Board want a Vision Statement because:

- They want a clever phrase to put in the annual report, on business cards and website?

- Everyone else has one, so we should have one, too?

- We've just paid a lot of money for a consultant who said we should have one?

- It seems like a good idea?

Or do they want a Vision Statement because:

- We need to focus on what our organisation is doing and should do?

- We value what our people think and want to include them in developing our future?

- We want to do things better?

- We want to move ahead and have our people committed to improvement?

Of course, you want these latter reasons to be the case.

Motivation is a critical aspect of developing a Vision. Vision requires passion and long-term commitment by senior management groups in your organisation in order to make it work. A Vision is the essence of what an organisation is and, therefore, needs careful consideration.

Leadership in building a Vision for an organisation is about facilitating structured discussion that draws out ideas, hopes and concerns. A proper process needs to be developed so that the channels of communication are clear, accessible and two-way.

Leadership in creating a Vision is also about the senior management groups in your organisation having a common understanding of the purpose of the organisation, and being committed to communicating and acting out the Vision across the organisation. This agreed-upon understanding needs to be tested and openly stated; simply assuming everyone shares the same commitment, values and ideals can cause confusion when creating a Vision.

Continues on next page

Inviting more people to participate in developing the Vision will make the process take a lot longer than just getting the Board to decide what your organisation's Vision will be. But the result of involving people across an organisation is that there will be shared understanding, more passion, and a commitment to achieving the Vision and Mission over the long term.

The project of creating a Vision Statement will need to have a "champion." This is someone who takes responsibility for keeping the project moving and for documenting and communicating progress. Usually, this is someone at a senior level in the organisation. This sends a message that the project is being taken very seriously by the CEO and Board. A working group could be established to share ownership of the project, which is a good way of involving people from different areas of the organisation in a common project that has enormous value to the organisation.

One of the most important skills a leader can have in this process is letting people speak and making time for them to express their views. Understanding the different personalities and styles of staff members is important in making sure everyone has a chance to participate.

Working groups can also play a role in leadership. Who in the group will make a big difference in how smoothly and creatively the development of your Vision Statement proceeds? Here are some questions you may ask yourself about the membership of the working group:

- Is there a trusted and influential staff member in the group?

- Should there be more than one staff member in the group?

- How many senior people do we want in the group?

- Do the members of the group get along well? What are the dynamics?

■ How representative do we want the group to be? Should it have internal and external membership?

■ If external people are in the group, will that stifle robust discussion?

■ Who would be offended if they were excluded from the group?

■ Who will chair the group? Whose style would get the best out of the group?

Generally, a group of no more than seven or eight people will be the most effective. Any more becomes cumbersome, and any less reduces the diversity of the group. Depending on the size of your organisation, a working group might have the following membership:

■ Chief Executive

■ One senior manager

■ Two or three staff members from different areas

■ A chairperson, who could be a professional facilitator brought in for the purpose

■ A person who uses your services or knows your business, if you want to involve external people

Before starting on the creation of a Vision, it is wise to take a look at the organisational environment you are in. Some questions that can help understand the environment are as follows:

- Does the organisation have a clear, documented set of Values, or is it assumed that everyone knows why they are doing what they're doing?

- Is there agreement at the senior level regarding what your organisation's Mission is? If you don't have a Mission Statement, does it matter?

- Are the Board, Chief Executive and senior managers open to broad consultation with people across the organisation?

- Are there already forums such as regular meetings where people can openly discuss issues?

- Are there good relations among staff and departments, or is there a sense of division regarding their functions or roles?

- Are change and innovation embraced across the organisation?

If the answer is "yes" to all of these questions, then you are more than likely in a good position to begin the process of creating your Vision.

If there are any "no" answers, then the development of a good communication plan will be even more important. The reason that a communication plan is important in this scenario is because the process of developing a Vision Statement needs a foundation of trust and openness to proceed effectively and with real commitment by everyone in the organisation.

Reviewer's Comment
Your Vision must be driven by your Chief Executive and have total senior management commitment. The communication of ideas throughout the consultation process will help to cascade this commitment down through your organisation and start to embed the spirit of the Vision. In this way, your Vision can start to have an impact on your organisation even before it's created.

Planning to Create a Vision

Planning is a vital part of creating a Vision. Like any project, having a set of aims and deadlines brings focus and helps establish the steps to be taken. Using a table can help clarify thoughts and set boundaries. The following table is an example.

Task	How	Who	By When
Talk about Vision project to Board	Next Board meeting	Chief Executive	5 June
Secure Board approval and support for project	Next Board meeting	All at meeting	5 June
Communicate results of Board meeting to senior management	Individual phone calls and face-to-face team meetings	Chief Executive and senior managers (the chair of the Board might also be at this meeting)	15 June
Introductory discussion and communication with staff	Develop schedule of consultative meetings and presentations	Chief Executive and senior managers	15 July
Establishment of working group	Appointment or election to group membership	Chief Executive	1 August
Staff consultation	Presentation at one or more meetings and regular written updates	Chief Executive, senior managers and working group	15 August
Communicate with Board to check general direction that the project is going in	Collate and analyse the results of the meetings, and submit results of meetings to Board	Chief Executive and senior managers	31 October
Draft written Statements	Meeting	Working group	30 November
Draft final Statement	Meeting(s)	Chief Executive and working group	1 February
Board presentation and approval	Board meeting	Chief Executive and perhaps chair of working group	15 February
Communication of Vision Statement and beginning of planning process	Meetings, newsletter, email, phone	Chief Executive, perhaps with Board chair and senior managers	Ongoing

ENGAGING YOUR ORGANISATION IN THE PROCESS

Engaging the organisation requires a similar approach as planning to create the Vision. Again, a table can help to measure and document your progress. This time, though, you will be working with a much wider group of people, and that means a much wider group of opinions and ideas. And not everyone is going to want to participate! This is where your work in building rapport and trust with staff will help facilitate a positive discussion.

An important point to make throughout the Vision project is that the Vision Statement is not just a slogan. You want to create a meaningful Vision Statement that actually helps people do their jobs better, creates unity and common purpose, and shows the world how unique your organisation is. There will always be a few who don't want to be involved, but the majority of people have a genuine interest in succeeding and achieving by being a part of something special and worthwhile. This is where a nonprofit organisation (NPO) has an edge – usually people are working there because they already believe passionately in what the organisation is doing.

Consultation can happen in a number of ways, and will usually include meetings where all staff (depending on the size of your organisation) will get together for robust discussion. In preparation for these meetings, it's a good idea to have some questions ready to stimulate discussion. You'll probably already have a point from which to start, whether that's a Mission, a set of Values or even a sentence or two about what your organisation does. These can be put up on the wall for reference.

After an introduction, the facilitator of the meeting might ask some questions of the group. Make sure the responses are noted. For example:

■ What do we do here at GreatOrg Inc.?

■ What would the world be missing if GreatOrg Inc. didn't exist?

■ What part does your specific job play in the success of GreatOrg Inc.?

■ Is there one word or picture that comes to mind when you think about GreatOrg Inc.?

■ Have any of your friends heard of GreatOrg Inc.? What is their impression?

■ What would you change about GreatOrg Inc.?

■ What would you change about your specific job?

Dissenting voices often inject the creativity required to get a lively discussion going. Healthy debate is beneficial in drawing out the important issues. However, hijacking meetings to suit individual agendas is a favourite pastime of the disgruntled, so the facilitator or chair needs to keep the meeting focused.

Some of the previously mentioned sample questions could invite some in the group to use the meeting to air their grievances. While it's reasonable to allow people to have their say, a good facilitator will know when to redirect the discussion back to the topic at hand. One way of doing this is to offer the disgruntled person time after the meeting to further discuss his or her problem with the relevant manager. Sometimes you won't be able to satisfy unhappy people, but as long as they are not disruptive, meetings should proceed without any major problems.

There are any number of possible questions that can be asked, and there will be an even greater number of responses. It's amazing how many different ways people can see an organisation. Therefore, this process will highlight the Values of the organisation that people agree are important as well as the role of the organisation in the world. By asking questions about people's specific roles and about the organisation as a whole, a picture will begin to form. Ideally, people will begin to see that their job is linked to others' jobs and that these jobs together make up the organisation. Now, some connections should be emerging.

Reviewer's Comment
Each stage of the development of your Vision helps to reinforce the Values behind it and to get your staff "on side." Again, letting people have their say and taking account of their ideas through consultation can motivate, excite and encourage creative solutions to challenges, before the Vision is complete.

LINKING VISION TO REALITY

One of the most common objections to Vision Statements is that they are meaningless to the everyday work that people do. This is not because Vision Statements are inherently meaningless; it's more likely that they have been imposed from "above," rather than developed with the participation of staff, and are seen as unrealistic.

Once you have consulted with your organisation, you'll probably end up with a short list of ideas about what the organisation wants to express through a Vision Statement. At this point, the working group might come up with two or three Statements as a starting point. These can then be taken back to the wider organisation for further discussion.

Discussions with staff groups will most likely be very lively. It is natural for people to want to express their views and realities of the world. This should be encouraged, but with some ground rules about respecting the opinions of others. Staff will look for ways to connect their everyday experiences in the workplace to the bigger organisational picture, and it is important that the process acknowledges this. However, the connections will be made clearer as the organisation works through the levels of planning, from the original creation of a Vision Statement to the development of individual goals.

Organisations are not usually completely democratic, but a good Chief Executive should be able to navigate his or her way through the consultation process to end up with a reasonably consensual Vision Statement.

Reviewer's Comment
Translating the Vision into individual goals can turn an apparently aspirational Vision into an achievable goal.

PLANS TO ACHIEVE THE VISION

Once a Vision Statement has been agreed on by staff and approved by the Board of Directors, you can begin to fill in the details of how the Vision relates to everyday work. This is done by developing Plans that relate to achieving your Vision.

Let's say that your organisation exists to raise awareness of dementia. Your Mission might be something like: "We are dedicated to creating better access to services for the diseases of aging."

Your Vision Statement might be as follows: "Within two years, we will have a suite of education programs that are widely used in our community."

Your Plans might naturally involve communication, so you could start with a list of things you want to achieve (outcomes), the things you are going to do to achieve them (actions), and the ways you will know that you have achieved them (measures). For example:

Outcomes	Actions	Measures
People know who we are and what we do	Create links in the community; develop a public relations and media plan; run a fundraising appeal	20 requests from local hospitals and general practitioners for information; positive mention at the local government meeting; five requests for media interviews
People know how to get access to services	Establish free phone line; produce simple brochure on available services; promote public seminar series	20% increase in phone requests for information; feedback on brochures tells us that the information is helpful; attendance at public seminars up by 30%
Awareness on dementia raised	Media advertising; seminar programs for schools, community groups and health professionals; seat secured on an important dementia forum	Evaluation forms and feedback indicate a 95% approval rate of our seminars; increase in community debate on dementia; government policy changed to improve services and funding

Continues on next page

Plans to Achieve the Vision

Within these Plans, the organisation can now see what needs to be done within departments and then by individuals. For example, to produce brochures, it will be someone's job to gather information, analyse it and write an appropriate summary. Funds will need to be allocated to pay for the brochure's production, printing and distribution. Budgets will need to be agreed on and managed. To run seminars, someone will need to organise a program, promotional plan, venue, catering, and audiovisual equipment. To change government policy, the Chief Executive will need to lobby and influence to get onto the right committees. All of these things and more will need to be done in order to achieve the organisation's Vision.

Department plans should guide each individual's written goals for the period. Individual goals are what lead everyday activities. When the next year comes around, individuals in the organisation will know exactly what they have done to contribute to the achievement of the Vision.

Reviewer's Comment
All elements of the department plans and individual goals should relate back to the Vision so that they are clearly seen as reinforcing the Vision and working toward reaching it.

COMMUNICATING THE VISION

If you have involved people across your organisation in the development of a Vision Statement, then communicating the Vision Statement within your organisation should flow easily from the consultation process. Having a nicely presented, framed document in common areas of your organisation is an easy and attractive way of communicating your Vision. An organisational event, or series of events, can help to keep people talking about the Vision and also introduce newcomers to it.

Having your Vision as a focus for orientation programs for new staff and Board members is also a good way of communicating your organisation's Vision, and sets the tone for what is expected of people when they come to work at your organisation.

Besides being a motivator for people inside your organisation, a good Vision Statement can act to attract interest and support from people in the community. A good example of this is in fundraising. Communicating the Vision through your fundraising program is a great way of getting your message across and showing people that you have a passion for what you're doing. Some ways of communicating your organisation's Vision might be to:

- Hold an event to launch a new program.

- Issue a press release to announce an exciting initiative.

- Have your Vision Statement printed on all informational materials and organisation stationery.

- Explain the Vision (and what's being done to achieve it) in the annual report.

- Regularly send out press releases about your organisation's achievements and explain how those achievements are contributing to the Vision.

- Use the Vision Statement to support funding applications and fundraising appeals.

Reviewer's Comment
Don't be afraid to use your Vision wherever and whenever you can.

So now you've got your Vision Statement in a nice frame in your office. What's next? Is that all there is to it?

When people begin to see results from following and developing their goals and department plans, they start to feel that they are truly involved in achieving the organisation's Vision. Regularly reviewing individual goals and department plans is a good way to acknowledge milestones and recognise achievements. Recognition is a key part of maintaining the passion for a Vision.

There are many ways of recognising the achievements of individual staff members, teams and the organisation as a whole.

Annual reviews
- How has the Vision Statement made a difference to the organisation?

- Are we living up to our Vision Statement?

- What do we need to change in our Plans to achieve our goals?

Annual/quarterly milestones
- When you have reached a particular goal or milestone, tell the story about it! Collect anecdotes and testimonials along the way.

Monthly reporting
- This is important for internal purposes to keep the momentum going. However, these need to be interesting or people won't read them.

Regular newsletters
- Updating achievements

Special events
- To celebrate milestones, why not hold morning teas or lunches?

Dissemination of feedback
- From outside the organisation, such as media clippings

People will remain committed to achieving the Vision if they know what their roles are, if they have goals, if they know what needs to be improved, and if they are rewarded and recognised for good work.

Reviewer's Comment
Failure to reward achievement and contribution can lessen motivation – so recognise and celebrate.

Evaluating the Impact of the Vision Statement

How do you know if your Vision has been achieved, or if it is doing what the organisation hoped it would? One way of evaluating its impact is to survey staff and people outside your organisation. Annual, anonymous staff surveys are very effective ways of finding out what people really think. If surveys are conducted independently, most people will usually feel quite comfortable in being candid in their comments. The results of the surveys can be used to gauge whether staff members have an understanding of the Vision, whether they believe in the Values of the organisation, and whether they feel committed to their work and to the organisation in general.

The simplest way to evaluate the success of your Vision is to refer to your Plans. Did you achieve everything and meet your measures? What else happened along the way? What didn't get done and why? What can be learned for the next time? What feedback have you had from your clients or their representatives? Was policy changed? Is your organisation considered at the top of its field in terms of quality and expertise?

The Plans are everything. They provide a clear path for getting the work done. As long as the Plans are linked, from the beginning, to achieving the Vision, then evaluating success should be a relatively simple task.

Reviewing and adjusting the Vision Statement should become part of the organisation's annual cycle of planning. In this way, individual and organisational goals and achievements are always kept current and evolving as the organisation evolves.

Conclusion

Vision Statements are not just slogans which have no practical relevance. A Vision Statement is a distillation of the people, ideas and values that make up an organisation. It is a way of expressing what an organisation is passionate about and what its aim for the future is. A Vision Statement summarises a realistic goal that can be applied to everyday work, and the successes toward its achievement can be measured and celebrated when reached.

It doesn't matter greatly what words you give to it, as long as the process enables you to get the results that you set out to achieve. If everyone can agree on what the organisation's values and purpose are, then everything else should flow from there.

A successful, meaningful Vision Statement is a progressive expression of the character, creativity and expectations of an organisation.